Stringpops
Film

Three pieces for flexible string ensemble
with piano accompaniment

SCORE + ECD of parts

Written and arranged by Peter Wilson

With many thanks to Janice Gillard for all her help

© 2009 by Faber Music Ltd
This edition first published in 2009
74–77 Great Russell Street London WC1B 3DA
Music processed by Jeanne Roberts
Cover design by Lydia Merrills-Ashcroft
CD recorded and produced by Robin Bigwood
Printed in England by Caligraving Ltd

ISBN10: 0-571-52925-9
EAN13: 978-0-571-52925-4

To buy Faber Music publications or to find out about the full range of titles available
please contact your local music retailer or Faber Music sales enquiries:

Faber Music Ltd, Burnt Mill, Elizabeth Way, Harlow CM20 2HX
Tel: +44 (0) 1279 82 89 82   Fax: +44 (0) 1279 82 89 83
sales@fabermusic.com   fabermusic.com

Contents

Put the CD in a computer to download PDFs of all the instrumental parts
and print out as many of each part as is needed:

Violin I
Violin II
Violin III
Viola
Cello
Double Bass
Open-string violin
Open-string viola
Open-string cello
Piano (and squash horn)

Put it in a CD player to hear the free audio tracks of the
piano accompaniments – ideal for rehearsals and performances.
Track 1 gives an A for tuning.

Sleeping Beauty Waltz

Pyotr Il'yich Tchaikovsky

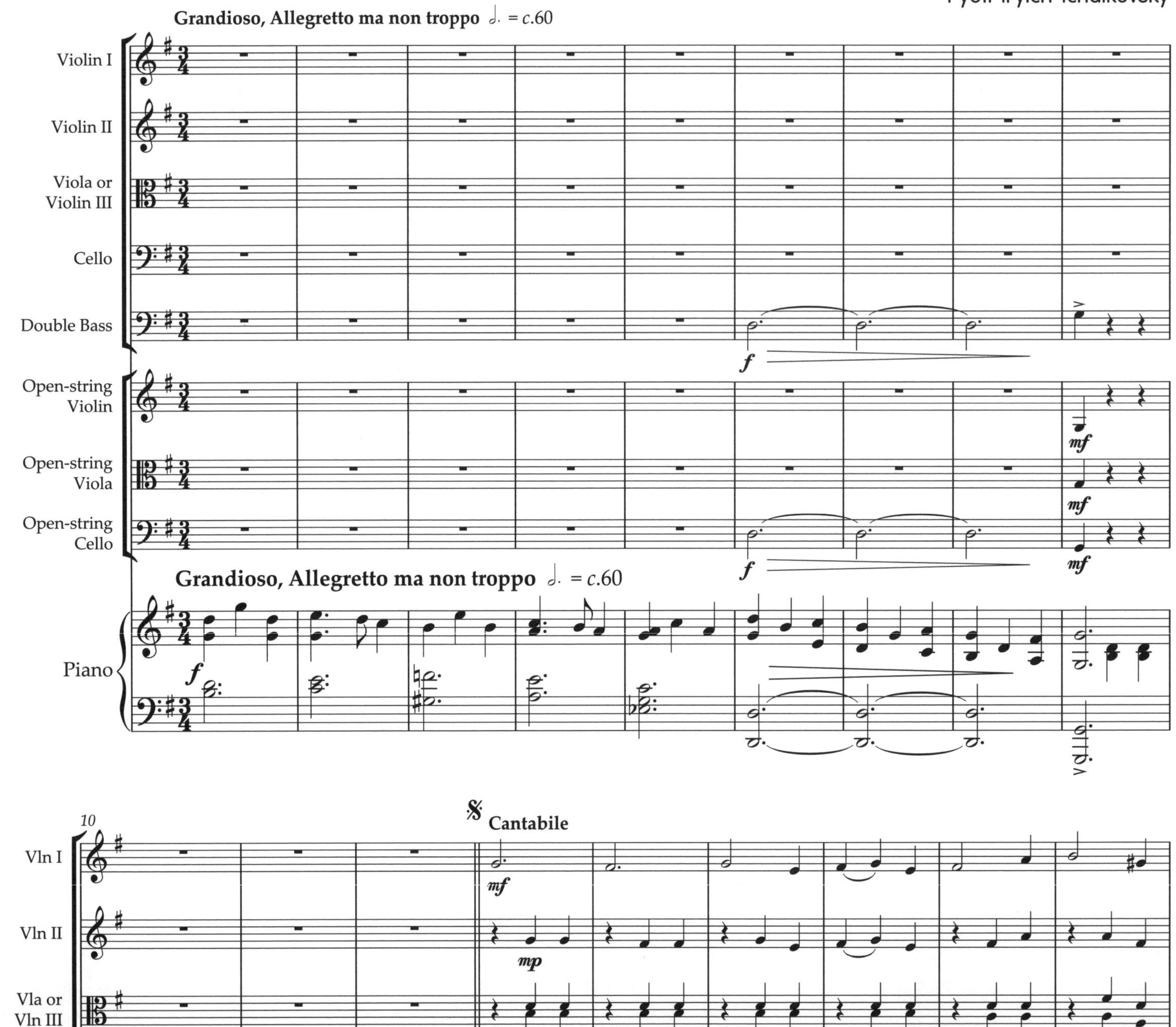

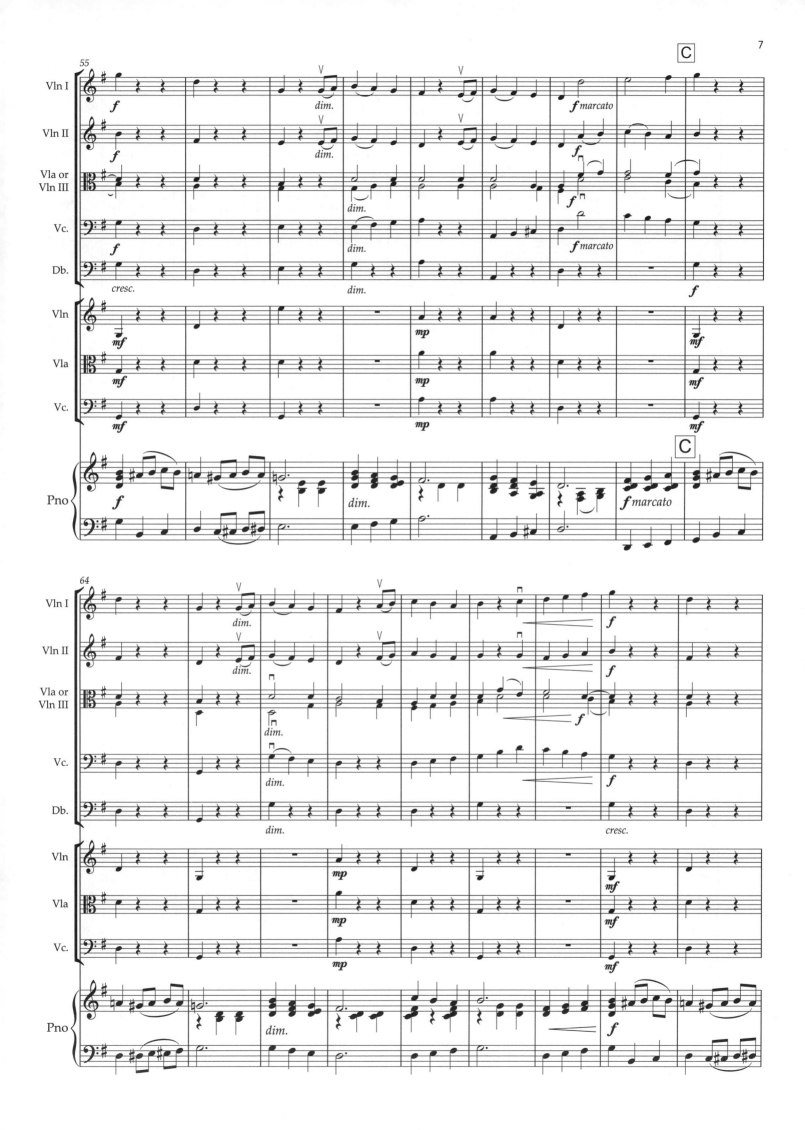

12

Beauty and the Beast

Words by Howard Ashman
Music by Alan Menken

16

Chitty Chitty Bang Bang

Words and Music by Richard Sherman
and Robert Sherman

ISBN10: 0-571-52925-9
EAN13: 978-0-571-52925-4

ISBN10: 0-571-52926-7
EAN13: 978-0-571-52926-1

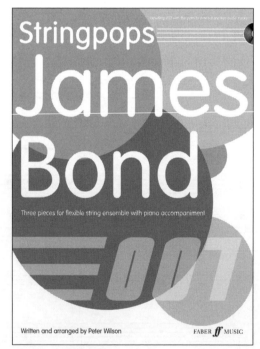

ISBN10: 0-571-52927-5
EAN13: 978-0-571-52927-8

ISBN10: 0-571-52928-3
EAN13: 978-0-571-52928-5

FABER *ff* MUSIC

To buy Faber Music publications or to find out about the full range of titles available
please contact your local music retailer or Faber Music sales enquiries:

Faber Music Ltd, Burnt Mill, Elizabeth Way, Harlow CM20 2HX
Tel: +44 (0) 1279 82 89 82   Fax: +44 (0) 1279 82 89 83
sales@fabermusic.com   fabermusic.com   expressprintmusic.com